ECHOES *of the* HEARTS

A Collection of
Heartfelt Verses

RAVI KUMAR YADAV

INDIA • SINGAPORE • MALAYSIA

ISBN 979-8-88883-286-8

Dedicated to all the enthusiastic readers who are fond of poetries…

Contents

Acknowledgements

The book “Echoes of the Hearts” is a collection of poetries written by me. All the poems are unique descriptions of the things I see and interpret differently. The poems jotted down in the book are stepwise mood changer and depicts how commonly we live but thinking about the same seems weird. I believe nothing is absurd, just the interpretation matters.

I am profoundly blissful while presenting my close-to-heart poems. I am immensely grateful to my family and friends, who felt the fire of my ambitions of publishing a collection of my works. The entire credit of this book goes to them as their motivation and love have always pushed me the entire way. It’s my first book and my first effort at parting my thoughts with people through this medium.

I hope you all will enjoy reading.

A Note for Readers

“Poetry becomes the breath, once you fall for it". Understanding makes them more touching and deep. Every line of the poem is like an embankment behind which the deep wells lie. Love for poetry can make your mind compatible with switching to any genre of the poem in the blink of an eye. Poetry is indeed a mood.

Here, in this book, you will get acquainted to the most mood-changing poems. What I mean by poetries is not just the beautifully woven words carrying rays of hope, love, depth etc, but a band of words that creates a mood of observation towards the strangest to the most common things around us. There is an accumulation of distinct meanings with varied readers, and this is the best part of a poetry. A poetry is not just free of judgments and reasons but is independent of every kind of bondages and limitations. This feature grants wings to the poetries. Consciously, it offers a sky full of extracts and subconsciously, it searches for the best content throughout the body. The darkest poetry may have the brightest lesson and the best poetries may come out of the worst experiences. So, in simple words, poetry is a freedom. A poet is as full of freedom as a reader and that's the essence of a poetry. Bringing to you my poetries that I wrote during my working days as a senior lecturer in Jharkhand government. As a teacher, I am not just a source of parting knowledge efficiently but am subjected to gaining the best experiences full of love, care, struggle, wishes etc from the students. The best thing about the book is that it yearns for freedom from the existing prejudices and norms and wants everyone to enjoy their life because they cannot opt for an another one. A balanced approach of hardwork and rejoicement makes a life worth it.

Read the poetries and observe the meticulous meanings in every word to get the best out of those.

About the Author

"Spills could hear your heart out and so does the tides; spills quietly make a listen while tides tend to react"

Ravi Kumar Yadav is the author of "Echoes of the Hearts". Presently, he is a lecturer in the Jharkhand government with additional in-charge of Principal. He wrote the book during his working days. He is vehemently fond of penning down his words to weave poetry. His additional areas of interest are singing, story writing, traveling, and teaching. He enthusiastically devotes his time in encouraging the writers of all spheres to get recognized for their distinctive works through the online platform – Being Omnific.

“

People don’t die of pain,
they die of intolerance

1

Dearly to Suicides

He committed suicide
The family excruciated the loss
Some cursed the boy's fear
While few were prompted to similarly escape life toss

For those few, life ahead became drudgery
Kept choice – either would be done or will die
Better than struggling, closing life's chapter seemed easy
And they finally choose escaping to sky

Leaving behind their innocent families
And the approaching good days after tough road
For biding away the mental unrest
With open arms, heaven's cart they board

Finally a trend and cycle of suicides
Rampant to turn out the sphere

Spreading terror far and wide
Others pretending " The air from somewhere.

So my dear future suiciders
Don't deal your life in seconds nine
Cause your moms bore pain for months
To heartily hug you and say 'Oh! dear child mine'

I know struggles of life are back breaking and heart sinking
But these are meant to fight
Not to sit lonely in dark preparing suicidal note
And fear till jumping from height

And so I ask and request together
Think a dozen times before indulging in such act
You may take away your soul but leave behind many
Who will immensely shed tears beating breast intact.

“

He, who experiences grief
Has no letter to write, in brief
They who really don't care for his steps
At his funeral, appear as celebs

“

A good human is not the one void of mistakes but the one carrying a load of regrets and still stepping with time. That’s what a soul longs for its mortal body.

2

Want of Soul

It's world
Nothing is going to last long
In this universe
Disaster has its own wreak
And we,
The tongue slippers for numerous dislikes
The action seekers possessing innumerable mistakes
The head frustrating overtime
The mind thinking beyond the reality
And eyes still expecting one's real or fake fame
Aren't out of the world
Our soul needs space
Where love forgives all flaws
And motivates for relishing the rest life
Relishing life is not restricted, not confined
And encouraging enough to regretting minds
Opening the door to dive beyond the ocean.

“

Do let love comprehend you what it is before you set for its rules that literally don't exist. It's a dandelion sacrificing to spread itself to bring charm to the world...

3

Interpretation of Deep Love

One day I woke up and found you beside me
So I started saying all that hoarding inside me
"Well, the last night I had cried equally to a lake"
and also explained that the words I said were not at all fake
So, dear, I began with your beauty
thinking it to be an "ideal boyfriend's duty"
and I shifted towards my words healing
that gave me a platform to express my feelings

<u>So I began again like –</u>
Oh! my dear, empress of my heart
How can I stay alive on being apart?
You have kept me awake from all the sleep
Isn't this what my love for you deep?

<u>She replied me blushing –</u>
My dear Adam, you are the first citizen of my heart
even I would die on being apart

But I am sorry to say that I had a nice sleep
So can't this be measured as my love deep?

And she gave a big pause to speak
Maybe she thought speaking out all could make our relationship weak
So I continued again, breaking the ice –
"When I think about you, I simply forget myself"
and your words helped me work like the magical elf
Also, when you ignored me, it made me weep
So, do become mine forever 'cause I love you so deep
She was hearing me all silent
About her praises and rudeness without turning violent
So I carried on –
My love! by the grace of God I got you
and thanks for filling my life with this attractive hue
Your anger always gives my cheeks lots of tears to seep
Why are you silent dear, approve all these as my love deep?"

So, she ultimately opened the shutter
and to the following words, she utter –
Oh, dear! I seek pardon, but I didn't weep
Nor ever gave tears to my cheeks so that they seep
However, I have lots of promises and will surely keep!

So now please approve this proposal as my love deep.
Hearing these words, I was hot with fire
I simply cursed her and titled her a 'love liar'
And before I could say another word
I was up by the door ring that I heard
Later, I realized that I was on my bed
Watching the dream all inside of my head
and the very moment, I stood up with all my force
Also, today after so many acceptances and rejection
I feel that I should have meant the mutual love definition
I feel sorry for I never knew that love mountain was so steep
and also because I failed to understand the real essence of the love deep!

Behind the hoardings of freedom, we are mentally in bondage of society and its unusually defined norms.

4

The Life

I was a puppet, puppet on this earth
I was made with surrounding's talks and
it was false that my mom gave me birth
'cause when I wanted to climb the tree,
its branches were cut
When I wanted to see the surrounding through windows
its glasses were shut,
When I wanted to get on terrace,
the ladders were misplaced
And when I wanted to wear sneakers
I was given bellies which were already tied and laced!
It was all because I was a puppet, puppet on this land
and my strings were not with my parents but
with the surrounding's hand!
My wings were cut,
when I wanted to fly
My tears were forcefully wiped,
When I wanted to cry

My pillow was snatched,
When I wanted to sleep
And I was called an actress,
When I felt to weep!
It was all for I was a puppet, puppet in the society
And I was made in the way they wanted to make me
treating me like a rubbish doll brutally.
Yes, I was tied up in the society's chain
and was forced to walk in the lamb's lane!!

I wish there was no pre-defined

Version of the term society to depend so blind

"Without bars I am held in cages"

Says the girl distraught through ages

“

Others' thoughts are being our limitations-

Do you believe?

5

Society and Me

Well! I was new to this world
And too young to know the term "society"
I thought it wasn't a mandate but
Their vision always held me guilty

For my every action
I had to be accountable
For their choices and faves
I sacrificed all I was capable

I was made to behave
As per their gender-based stereotype
Or else threatened or harassed emotionally
For getting a societal wipe

No matter what I was fond of
Their reaction was forever on priority

How awful they'll talk of myself
If I consider my anything pretty

I was of belief: the world is my family
And a great source to support
But true acquaintance was marked
When parents told me their deeds of all sort

But I am never gonna be their subject
Would rather break their prejudices
To let the future, not suffer, to accomplish
Their exuberant wishes!

“

I am weak and withered
Like the purple in the vase for beauty
Jealousy is their custom disposition
And discouraging is their undefined duty

"If I had gifted her wings, she won't have flew to the world beyond humans", Realized

6

Untraced Reproach

She wished for wings
They gave her rope
She needed support
They destroyed her hope
She has enough potential
Looked for scope
Nobody was ready
To part their cope
She tried climbing a cliff
They pushed her off the slope
Now they sit to curse her
for she hung herself with the rope!

“

If love was interpreted right,

There would have been no quarrel or fight

The true meaning would kindle a light

And there was no darkness before and after night...

7

Love Beneath Chapters

Love was never transparent
It was always a shy worm
That eats away your judgments
And lends you purity for someone
Love isn't the venus alone
It lies in its shine out of love for self, indeed
And even if there were no rings
Saturn would never forget the warmth of their presence
Love is known as scars with which the moon proudly shines
And even if it was meant a fall
Love was the coming spring
In the green wide meadows
Every burnt paper was white
And every phase of the moon is bright
Love is lovely and indeed a bond
That is unconditional, unwavering
And undoubtedly unquestioning.

“

What if every person was good in this world?

This poem never existed......

8

World of Betrayals

The world, a liar
A betraying buddy
Tells and teaches lie
Just to keep others in custody

Indifferent to others' life
Who contending for their rights
No morals knock their minds
Persist with their dross fights

Love of life is drudgery
For them the best is revenge
Others' sufferings and injuries
To their mindset, fails to change

A vast sea of humanity
Lacks the trustworthy
Their deception and ignorance
Makes their heart swarthy

“Oh, he is yelling out of pain and blood!”, the poor mother of the murdered child cried in her nightmare.

9

The Best Spirit

Lost in the betrayal
of darkened heart
The best spirit
Lost its frenzied part

Indifferent to the poor's feed
Treacherously making others mutt
Thinks everyone as their slave
Brainless, steel tendon robutt

Just pants on shudder
Thinks others' life a perpetuating bubble
I feel they're too hideous
For exhausting others in trouble

Enough's enough but
Feels nice on other's shrieks
Own groanings are served
For others, have brutal, ruthless tricks

Their words quiver persist
Nitwatness loses in the mist
I feel, God! what a shuddering life
Fails to balance on the tones of fife

She had heard the soft voice
Waving out through the dark skies
The meadows turned like her body
And the desperate soul left for cries

"What are these cinders about, dad, that immensely beautifies the wrecking fire?"

"Dear we fuel these fire out of our shedding values" Dad explained...

10

Cinders in Flame

Life is relentless
and full of hardships
Life simply means
a slender keeps

Pretty hideous it becomes when
danger comes to a man
his courage cinders in flame
and thinks of elation which can

The honesty cinders in flame
when all becomes a blackguard
and immensely shake the goodness
which was left too hard

Infernal deeds of a crazy
impertinence words of imposters
cinders the fraternity in flame
lending persistence to divisions by ancestors

"

Power or love?
She opted for both...

"

11

The Power of Love

"Life then death"
is the pure slogan
but "died to live"
looks perplexing and fun

The relentless life goes on
its the common humdrum
but love and loving ones
gives the best on being sum

Love has a dexterous mystery
Even the lost one frantically gets victory
the loving heart spreads far
though gingerly on the obstinate bar

The contours of love
echoes on hill
and its power propels
with pitches and shrill...

"Hear me and go, Wishing for no sympathy, no space, and no worry", the orphan died in the corner of the lane...

12

A Threatening Request

Hey! The Passing you
Just turn the side invisible to you
Here I am shouting strangely
A wild cry that you would just feel
And you'll feel like calling a crowd
The crowd, you know
For not softening my wounds
But to display all, like a show
A wild request that may seem like a threat
Just bind me in shackles
And turn me behind bars
But do donate me a visible side
A visible corner to sit
To sit and cry with bloody tears
And exhibit my lamentable sacrifice
The sacrifice that yearns for satisfaction
And liberation contently

Behind bars I'll yelling unworldly phrases
That won't affect you but express me
My pitiful lamentation within
That the world failed to feel
And I'd liberate unknowingly

Bowing his face, he sat on knees

In the dark, breathless box without breeze

Waiting for someone unknown to reach

To threaten and scare the mild man with creech

"Bringing for you the beauty of good dreams", the hallucination disguised to deceive...

13

The Hallucination

She was staring at me
With those frightful red eyes
that may have lost innumerable days of sleep
The most serrated sharped teeth ever
I witnessed the ugliest and the most odious face
and the sudden of her appearance
O, God! I jumped a foot off my bed
falling in the murk of my room
She was about to take away my breath
and the terrible intolerable shout she roared
The rough blows were choking my neck
and I turned unconscious out of trepidation
With the horrifying dusty storm, she started approaching me
and I panic-stricken predicted for no life the another
second
And now that she was the closest to me
her flash broke my tone

and I opened my eyes paining in death
I could feel the scars of the scare
but could find no such scene
All that I wildly saw
Was the power of the dream
Yet I conquered it and am alive
To look for another hallucination

If suffering had a face
Indeed that would be a nightmare
Too light to catch and breathe
And too dark to scare

Rightly comprehended –
why real had an opposite?

14

I Was Wrong

Passing three decades of my lifespan
Even now am not experienced to recognize a man

I had believed on his every tricky act
and trusted his every words like fact

His tears are enough to mark him right
Wait, 'I witnessed he himself had started the fight'

For such black hearts, the justice is unjust
For him his possessions possess priority first

Their is an evil behind every pretty face
Every corrupt is a winner in the worldly race

There is wickedness behind every tear
Beneath many mind opening lectures, there are thoughts mere

Here, no lotus rises out of mud
but sighs of relief for hiding faults shedding blood

Game of emotions is marked as life
No apologies for mistakes but a suicidal note with knife

Every sweet word hides roughness of the taste
Escaping his guilts, every fake emotions are off like waste

I, the victim of the hypocritical natured being
have ruined my beliefs of everything

Now that I remember the memories of my old days
I say, "I was wrong analyzing his vivid cheating ways."

“

Justified words too need amend

And incoherent ones need to comprehend

The blues scattering reached the end

And the horizon loses its blend

“

The dead being impatient
Darkening the wilds of the towns...

”

15

Sorry to Die

I had been pondering onto
the quests of my life
the conqueror me still embarrassed
for the impatient turnout disguise
holding upon the breaths
cursing those tough ways
entering the addiction
another time befriending the dead man
the one out for shouts and shrieks
and sinking within the cell of useless efforts
burying my sins under the holy church
and sacrificing this life
to challenge the poor me, the weak soul
writing in the hand "Sorry to die"

"What have you saved out of your sacrifice?", the disciple asked the monk

"A hundred lives", smiled the monk...

16

Saving a Hundred Lives

He left for dark leaving the light
Stood for alms leaving the castle
He had learnt every step is one's own
He chosen going far from all his known
Cause his perceptions went ahead
Pondering"I may be a force"
My preferences may be a pain
For those very close to me.
His choices could hurt the knowns
His words could hit the knowns
His actions could tense the knowns
His reactions could kill the knowns
So came up with one way
He left all and walked away

“

If “double-faced” was simply literal,
They would emerge out of the social mindset......

17

That Double Faced Man

I was lonely walking at night
A little afraid, yes right

For every step, I watched all side
One way of relief, I had no one to abide by.

My house was at far
I could hitch no buses or car

To my scaring eyes, the distance increased
I walked roughly on the road greased

I had a bag with a phone inside
But I couldn't call for the battery had died

I preferred walking fast in silence
Cause dark had 'to hinder and scare' license

It wasn't cold but I felt cool
Suddenly I saw a man near the school

He looked terrifying with mustache on cheeks
While I was stepping, he gave peeks

I could feel tense in my mind
Then he started approaching me from behind

I tried walking faster without turning back
With a heaviness on my shoulder, I saw a hand black

His masked face, dull and dark
The night more horrified with dogs bark

I forgot the words out of fear
All seemed to blur in my eyes full of tears

Before I did take another step
He asked, "May I help?"

I was a bit relaxed to say
"No, I will walk my way."

"By the way don't try to chase!"
"Who knows where you'll change your phase"

"Oh! Dear girl, I am a man of grace"
"See my heart, don't visit my face"

"I'll be at far, and will shield"
"And take you safely across the field"

"How can I trust a stranger and especially a man"
"It's up to you, if you want you can"

I took his grace and walked all together
At that moment I was a bird ready with feather

Fortunately, with his mercy, I was at my house
All right, in front of my guiding spouse

His face unveiled at the time
Giving my thoughts a boost sublime.

“

‘Gifting a present and granting a potential’

Love vanishes the boundary...

18

Gifting You the Sun

My love, you know
You mean me my whole
Cherishing all your lovely moments
I would satisfy my soul…

For you my darling
I would collect the reasons to smile
And bestow you the events of your choice
To adore your happiness all that while…

My dearie, with a grand welcome
I would breathe you in
And dote on all your imperfect perfections
Holding in my hand your beautiful chin…

And snapping your best shots
With all your alluring poses done
I would shower you with all the radiance
While gifting you the splendid sun!

“

Deeper the love,
Stronger the roots of agony

19

The Agony of Solitude

I read and tagged for a while
To lose his memories I travelled a mile

Neither I could rage nor weep
Even my painful eyes refused to sleep

Mind got blocked and heart fell ill
For it needed nothing more to get kill

No recreation worked a bit
My pain could call no medical kit

This hearty wound, deeper than vale
I could be relieved by no tale

Though foody but hardly I could eat
And this heart started skipping the beat

My breath was full of sorrow
Hope denies for his comeback tomorrow

I lost acquaintance to my emotions
And my broken tears could be healed by no lotions

Completely overwhelmed by solitude
Now sitting heavily with hands nude

He left my hand and it became load
Regret left me with no lively mode

Nothing left, I feel to suicide
No responsibility left to be abide

Tears are not forgetting their way
Corner of my eyes; their abode to stay

Now dark seems my only mate
For him now I am a subject of hate

Now his every memory will turn me bony
I wish death to hug me and my agony…

“

Picking up the broken pieces of my heart
I sat alone to hear its echo
My solitude brought me a coffin
And my garden scooped up a grave
With the ugliest flower to sow

“

“I am dying everyday for my livlihood”, the distressed man narrated his tale

“Don’t let the last death approach you”, the monk said with a smile...

20

The Last Suicide

I led a several lives
You know, all with healing hope
The reason,
I would never understand
Cause I've led the last suicide
Hope, fate, desire and soul
All stood sulking unknowingly
The reason,
I would never understand
Cause I've led the last suicide
One cured with shinning eyes
Second time, the luck awaited
But again and again I broke within
All hope became hopeless
The way, I had to go on
I strangely stepped back
And where the cliff ended sharply

I strongly stepped ahead
The last thing I perceived
"I won't get back from this well"
For all your help, my angles
I am heading towards hell
The reason, I would never understand
Cause I've led the last suicide……

“

My peak saw my hundered deaths
Some in dark and some in light
For now the snow melts so dazzling
For getting the pain stacking sight

“

Bury the regret with your mistakes in the past itself, don't let them murder you a dozen times...

”

21

A Painless Murder

I was murdered a dozen times
All that was painless
But enough to darken my mind
And squeeze my red heart
He held the whip but cursed me
And the unused whip lost its hit
He opened fire but I wasn't burnt
Though felt the extremest heat
Surrounded by icebergs I got no frostbite
But my heart was trapped in ice
He ruined my lovely made world
And I was broken within
He took away my relatives though I was not harmed
But rooted out my reason to live
No bruises, no bleeding, I was safe and alive
Though was alone with my mistakes and regrets
I was murdered a dozen times!

“

Fall in love with nature, it won’t leave to die out of lonely pain...

22

Alone

I would wail looking at sky
to let my cry reach too high
and call the clouds upon to rain
to furnish a rainbow to my pain

My tears would let the flowers to bloom
enchanting fragrance to spread in my room
I wouldn't let anyone to close the door
to let the spray flourish more

The dirt of my hardworking hand
would ask for no abode on land
it will love to be flowed
and weariness vanish in the air blowed

The rising hope in grasses spry
I won't let them hear my cry
I would rather hug a tree
to let my despaired mind be free

I wish no love to be showered on me
for unlocking my expression I would offer no key
I would lie on grass green
everyday to mark the stars as seen

I don't expect to be fed by spoon
and would sing no lovely rhyme for moon
its shattered image behind the trees
will bestow my fire cool breeze

If I would feel to sing a song
I would approach the forest throng
if my heart sinks in thoughts deep
I would distract it with a loud beep

I wouldn't let butterflies to sprinkle me charm
I would simply queue them next and cause no harm
Now I won't have bookmarks of memories to be cherished
I'll be too far to let you know that I have perished
You know I wouldn't let anyone to blame
from my life to rub off your name
only I would tell you I choose darkness to moan
and now nature is little mine for you left me alone…

“

So how one hand can refuse the clap
And a leg refuse to step ahead
Becomes my part and breaking me apart
He offered my death, soilful spade

“

“Death listens no cries of pain and no plea of misery”, daddy teaches his son

“I would befriend the death and request him to inform before the hugging the humans to the darkest world”, the son said out of innocence……

23

Death: A Deal of Life

The wounds of death
though are alive,
is treated as a ceremony
for liberation of elements five.

The body burns in fire
but its works are essence of air
past, present and future inculcated
chances to remember are uncertain and unfair

Every beautiful moment of life
rests in scenario out of smoke
and the bad ones experienced
fall on ground as ash, the earth soak

His good works are message
to the world insane out of greed

and the one committed out of evil
propels within people for selfish feed

The belongings are then the earth's waste
for no museum exists for unique man
his sufferings and devotions are laid
for his immortal journey, humans have no plan

Pain may be excruciating for his family
but does not forever persist
In front of lamentation of his death
mist out the fact "light comes out of mist".

I was merciless at the fact
They had to leave their entirety
From the land, they had to disappear
Gradually losing their whole entity

“

The most serene vibe I find here. At the home of all unknown side along fetching up fresh breath.

24

The Serene Melody of Nature

The golden air without hits
Slightly moving over the head
Only the chirp of the wagtail
And the shrilly cicadas

Lying in the shade, I
Jocundly of the tree
Which sheds leaves as for love
And makes my pensive mind free

The lake along the untenured fence
Merrily flowing on gentle slope
And the seedlings nearby
Rise as the ray of hope

The above clouds float a brake
For an angel to come down

To make me sleep
Without tensions on crown

This serene melody of nature
Is opulent of height
And the peace it bestows mesmerizes
At several of eye-catchy sight

“

The cloudless sky echoes with chirp
Of the vibrant beautiful birds
Made this poet lose himself to love
Giving an ethereal blend of words

“

Who said love is between bodies, it’s within body with its soul.

“Daddy, can a person really love himself?”, She asked

“Yes, she did”

25

Left No Reason

When you'll meet her
You'll find a satisfied soul
Cause she left no reason
Not a mark of any depression or hole

She was the happiest of all
Cause her love was 'she'
She cared herself and her every choice
Pinned up everything that made her glee

She beautified her garden with flowers
And cooked a wide, to eat
She was pleased talking to herself
And ardently offered herself the seat

Standing a fore, she asked the mirror
To choose, for her, the best dress
With every sun, she furnished a rose
To herself to impress

Laying merrily under blue sky
She chosen the brightest star
With her eyes slightly closed
She built fantasy so far

She gifted herself every birthday
The crown of radiance leveling up
And she tightly hugged herself
Every time she got a hiccup

It's not that she hated the world
But wanted an honest life without
About the world's dishonesty, hatred and violence
Very early, she had heard a man's shout

She wasn't alone, had befriended the nature
Surrounded by birds, flowers, sky and trees
Every memory that she snapped
Cherished her and her friends' cheese

Now that she's no more alive
Still her coffin is the most serene
In the darkest, terrifying graveyard
Nature bestowed her the loveliest scene…

“

Now the grave smells too sweet
And no scary feeling comes across
She had a true desperate love for herself
That could not be opposed with a toss

“

Silence, there’s the poet talking to death!

”

26

How I Wanna Call Death??

I won't urge you to silently and peacefully make me fall
I won't either insist you to take me away painlessly
Dear death, my only friend, to whom my entity is the last
I would never request your to hug me warmly
I have befriended you and indeed it was the record of fate
Yet I won't die to fall in you dark lap
You'll will accurately present to see me passing away
Hey my bestie, don't be tensed, in fact I would meet you the way you want
With your desires at priority, I would breathe my last breath
All that I would wish for is being isolated at the end of my chapter
So I won't hurt the upcoming days of the new lives
You are most welcome, I would definitely wait to meet you at time right
And as willing for long, would sit alone on corner readily

To meet you enthusiastically and wave a good bye
To this true and real role of the show
I would love my death and interim would mark no wailing of bereavement…
Indeed a serene death

Death is blind, sees no good place
Death is breathless everywhere
He, who's afraid of it, deems to be the one
Of truly nowhere

If any decision did not have a permanent effect...

27

The Shine to the Dark

Being sandwiched for being single or not
I possessed no experience of mine
Where I enjoyed the laziness of singularity
Hope for a partner led me lose shine

A late sleep, indeed no tension
A warm sleep missing her arm
Lately awaken nobody to worry or scream
Hugging teddy to adore her charm

Fortunate to relish all the delicacies alone
Interim without a partner, all turns insipid
Half percent still balancing both weights
Still consoling myself to turn to examine experience vivid

Turning now to watching a movie
Romantic ones yearns for her Presence

And horror movies make need of her tight hug
Yet when single am not worried for extra expense

With her around, surrounding would be aromatic
Though singularity would capture no under cause
So have been doubting my future to be
Of befriended one, would I repent for what the past was

Am in fact, a struggling man
Caught in the exclusive cage of dilemma and doubt
Am not in way of ruining the lives ahead
Cause it's life, not what the story was about

In fact a sin would weight my head
If I turn wild on her little tender heart
I am indeed unsure what I truly long and need
As the time of building up future has pushed a start..

I am happy right now
Once glad, the other moment weep, they bark
Am unsatisfied whether my fragile option
Would push my shine to dark…

“

Neither a flower nor a thorn of it
I’ll be the soil to hold everything
I’ll have both of accept and refuse
Neither will scatter nor furnish anybody wing

“

I am facing you and the truth is
behind, shy and unrecognized –
Don’t let this ever happen

28

If Losing Trusted Love

Love being the most influential
I am afraid of withholding the same
Well not in touch now, am solitude
Cause for betrayal, I can't just turn to blame

Still unveiling my innermost feeling
To know myself better before I fall
Am still unknown to the person I'll love a lot
Because love isn't a just feeling at all

Making myself comfortable with the person
I would wish to share my whole
Embodying – love isn't just between bodies
But too is the emotional connection of the soul

Have heard of many stories
People die loving the one who never knows

I wish within my circle there's nobody such
Cause I wish no unintentional hurt to those

Among the crowd, I have been so fading
Of the story I have heard, whether is applying itself in me
I would rather hug that person
For carrying this heavy feelings sea

Or else if known from otherwise
I would end up curtailing my mind
Though unknowingly but hurting the one
Who has been in role of such kind…

“

The ashes unfuel
Once the head feels down
The fact that she'll hold me through dark
Just rusted my crown

“

The mercy being speechless between the devil and the deep blue sea and the poet picking up the miseries.

29

In the Middle of Lane

Heart broken, eyes intoxicated
And mind determined to suicide
Words hid inside and face full of tears
Nobody there against this decide

I was meant to stand till death
With the speedy train approaching soon
In the night, likely to fall as corpse
To shine deadly in the bloody moon

Hope now left for the train only
To cut me apart and forgive my fear
In the daylight however, I took no chance
In the crowd to ridiculously appear

They would deride on saving my risk
Layering me with another reason

Making me more insane to die close
Waiting for no change in season

Suicide is my proclivity
They fail to understand this
In their eyes, my weakness is pulling me
Lending me no space of bliss

Particularly to escape I opted this path
In the whole sea of darkness
They were seeking for trace of wrath
I was still unknown to their mere politics

'Was still being full of regret to spread this dare
But they wanted it to happen or to save
To laugh at unleashing expectation of care

With trembling legs, I stood chest a front
To lose myself to the air at short
Would now look for no dream
To confirm my will of death; abort

And as I'll escape to sky
I would never see down to earth
At no condition I would risk again
To here as a man take another birth…

“

That dark was a pleasure

Cause life was on end

Mistakes would be forgotten and he'll be free

Of the miserable days he spend

Disclosing his eyes forever to not accepting nature

The soul didnot want to leave

Mind was determined but heart was in fix

As a living one could bring goodness as sieve

For a body that strives
There's a mind that thrives
To create and conquer
A day of pleasure!

30

Striving for a Pleasing Day

I was tapering for the last pleasure
I thought of having my ambitions measure
To those who have relished life
Having described it as melodious as fife
And looking at them I was heedless to mine sad days
And no wonder, out of such feel, I was seeking for the ways
Yet I could not find one
For me the mixture always was separated like swan
When I looked at grass, they were spry though small
But this little motivation was not all
I moved to nature to see if God was really great
Biting my fingers, I began to sweat
And I, from then was allegiant to his art
By bestowing niche to all those part
And as I observed his love so invisible yet vast
And poor me was wailing for that gone in past
I was yet to kindle high

Cause my age was not a matter to shy
Book of life has similar pages till end
And how I write it would give it a sharp blend
I had no reason to console this freak
I was now no more a weak

He did not strive
He waited and waited
Till the edge of impatience
To live the day he wanted

“

There are people who die for our sake...

31

Love in Matter of Words

Every bangle tinkling with grace
has broken beating upon the face
Those eyes carrying sparkle of hope
now stone-heartedly bearing the hazard to cope
such sight has turned waiting impatiently unending
forcing hearts to voice cries most excruciating
jewels that used to adorn the celebration of his presence
have been faded out of his true essence
waiting to hug him tightly after a long
rather mercilessly pushed to bid goodbye the rest life long
Every letter that frantically pleaded for his return
has been spilled in ink to mourn
she agonizing when world prayed and praised his valour
now dispelled from beauty like a wandering sailor
"once, just once open eyes to inform about the go"
deadly in front of posthumously body, she made her last bow
"fires of your pyre flourishing for your courage high"
melting the soul within me, flaming my life in ashes to sky

“

There is a hope
In your dark room
Stand up blind-folded
And start searching
Let the past help you
Observing every corner...

32

Bad in Hate the Same Out

I'm a bit over thinker
Of my past beating it dark
And indeed every few hours
I would do the most unwanted cry
Full of tears of repent
Watching the horrific scene
Of the rapid time walk
Giving me no time to get breathe
Of the moment I lived and will live
However, my nostalgia
Hates the wailings of out
Introverted till the extended age
Of my air like life
I'd sit once to count the days
And aware myself of the remaining part
To rise below the sun

"

A flow of memory...
Shh! The poet is dreaming...

"

33

Painting My Dream

The black to get cover of sky
The green though dark to depict nature
Yes I had the beauty of depth
And a light hand so warm in look
Even more convincing to my parched soul
And I saw myself running blindly
As if a chase to someone I lost
A note in my hand, my hand in air
And the air so luke on my yearn
The run so rapid leaving drops of tears
Making my every single thought a milestone
And so soothing so warm and so healing
The same hand I felt back
Even the water from clouds
Could quench thirst of my throat and not heart
So sitting down a mysterious tree

With graceful branches and non rustling leaves
And a magical lake nearby where instead of fishes
The dead desires floated with the curvy waves
And the time, the perfect one
To let me think of finding out my one
My drawing paper left blank

“

She sat with a brush
To disclose her will
Turned white into vibrant
Smudges of thrill

“

The True Imprint is all about...

34

The Imprints of My Scars

That night,
I fought my sadness
I fought my pain
I fought my anxiety
I fought my depression
I fought my doubt
I fought my criticisms
I fought my limitations
I fought my fears
The next day,
I found my body
With the imprints of my scars

“

Still we layer with bands of lies......
That’s us turning blackguards

”

35

We Know the Truth

They made it to cheat intentionally
And accentuated it naturally occurred
They turned to twice their craze
And harassed the other for right
They killed the bird with triggering words
And held it suicide undistinguished
They sang for the goodness, oh no,
But to gain attention of unwanted sympathy
Still the truth we write
Cannot be foretold with boldness in crowd
But staying in weaved huge layered shell
Because one knows the right
And the wrong has defence tight

“

We wait for the stars to shoot and never believe in reaching them...

36

Hope That Seems Hopeless

I admired how the darkened Sun
Again shines with hope that dies
I made myself a bit to it
But devastating were my inner cries

I admired birds that flew with freedom
And height above all reach
Yet when I turned to their full hope
They soon leave at night for the darkest teach

And yet am going to gain a little peak
To the nature that seems so hopeful
Unlike what my mind predicted
Everything turns downtrodden with dark and dead...

“

Taking in pain and sighing out
words is my way of poetry

37

Years

All this era meant to burn me
Heat me up and never
To my belief a warm up
I have been through long years
Of unjustified wars
Mockingly lying behind the doors
Means to the future me
Although if I was brave enough
To fight my past
My past seemed a miraculous beauty
Where my mistakes have awakened me
And are still to warn me
There's none of your records
Even if it was you and your past
All this beauty is rising with time
Piling up lessons to preach in heaven
To the unborns Or the deads
Well my past wasn't me

But my older version
Full of unsafe and irrelevant stuffs and acts
And still am reverent for it
To secure my future
Years of unknown penance
And decade of building
Now are witnessing
The distinct versions of me

Thats a dream to gift
The time, my ages hence
To let it know how priceless
Could be the mortality essence

“

That’s love

”

38

The Fear of Losing You

I would weave new days with you
I would recall my memories with you
That would be the most heart melting evidence
You would never investigate
It would be harder for you to watch
My tears of pain
May be you know I did a weep
But the heat of sympathy for me
Would be forever in me
Can't hold you but can feel pleasure
Memorizing that
Can't hear you but can talk to you virtually
You may not know you are the reason
And the goal of my life
And I can't ever think of losing you
I am here in front of you, do mark the
Most chaotic mind

I am dying fighting within myself
With regret and aspirations
With present and future
With past and memories
You may not know I am the most fearful person
I can't ever think of losing you…

What pokes my heart everyday
Is watching you go, me being worthless
As dew falls off the leaves
And the approaching universe lifeless

“

There is no drop
That cannot shine
Yet they have a fall
From the darkest sky...

39

Mind or Mountain

The peak touches the sky
And its foot so deep and wide
Would I make mind to win its peak
Or the fear of height would let me abide

I dream of mountain so unreachable
But in dream I marked its defeat
I made up my mind to ignore its strength
And stepped gathering up my heat

“

There is beauty in everything created by nature

The best example is you!

40

While Thinking of My Imperfections

The morning so voracious
With the melodious vibes of chirpy
Little birds
And adding to the beauty was
My rise up
When the sun's rays glammed
Up my face
And I started my day, humming
Stability of my entire structure
Dancing gracefully
Happiness requires no step to learn
And dear me, unknowingly was
Vibing all along the beautiful day
As if it was the last day of my life
So reaching the mirror, I confidently
Made my head up
And no less than a blink of eye

I got non-plussed on this ugly dye
Indeed the mirror was reflecting me
So dark truth intangible, but need
No witness to last and packing up all
My imperfect beauty
I danced the most unstable one
Within so jaded
But couldn't pretend my glad
Poor me! That's the will of the nature
Wanding you this hopeless beauty
And in the dreams
When fairies were at far
Maybe the reason was my dark luster
I asked nature if it was unjust
And she didn't made a hesitation
To aware me to love the imperfect me
Love so deep that perfections fade off its beauty
And so was me
Not thinking but thanking my dark beauty

“

Like the candle lightens with imperfect flame

And the imperfect clouds bring pleasure to parched land

Why me being shameful for my ugly looks?

Those imperfections grant me a personality grand

“

Born to create history or repeat history?

”

41

Beyond the Old Me

The day brighter like my devotion
And sun distanced as my destiny
I am a step before the threshold
That would indeed take me beyond the old me
Cause the time has turned me too young
To get on my hardworking days
Time is counting on my days to look for the modified me
Raising myself too above to obviate my nostalgic sense
Above the clouds to ignore the ground of dead leaves
A single person in dark crowd
Where every warmth and comfort trespasses
And I working like a labour of my dream
To reach that only vision
Not waiting but watching progress I am going through
Where for every hurt, Mom's veil is folded
And friend's sharing is splitting like marbles

The sea dead thinking for the grave like life ahead to reach the heaven
Right, but bitter not the taste but the road
Taking me with intense ups and downs
Tragic losses that only I will bear
And still doubted for that single gem

“

The bugs are away from the plants they ruin

And still the plant dances elegant

The ruins too flow somewhere

No regret of being a vacant

42

This Was My Fate

Indeed for society I was a liability
Finding my indulgence in household only
For little mistakes, was condemned so brutal
Their mere perceptions biding me lonely.

Their superiority was tradition
A tradition laid in the curse of knowledge
They preferred prioritizing their entity
Discriminated females to hug this weigh

Since childhood, I was subjected to restrictions
Then to another world, was confined
Not a trace of opportunity permitted to my life door
And was ridiculously derided for lagging behind.

As per ritual, was departed from my beloved home
Where I had the most redolent childhood memories to keep

the in-laws house, where my every step was fearful
Overwrought by nostalgia, got no tranquil sleep.

Accentuated as a member, but considered a burden
Unknowingly, I became the matter of their grief and rage
Feeling myself so suffocated within
This manly prepared exclusive cage

The scene turned wild when
I was taken as a puppet and played persistently
They used up my body cruelly until was emotionally dead
Mercilessly was thrown out of use, damaging me physically and mentally

At such height, winds of loneliness fading off my soul
I had no care taker to wait
Yet empowering myself repeatedly to deal this challenge
Sadly, still they say "this was my fate"

Who is women?
The visible toy - use & throw
Find and play, see and ignore
The uncivilized men said in row

“

The game of threads...Beautiful

The threads in the hands of the society...Disastrous

43

Puppet of Society

When born at a place
I was given a blank mind
Before this what the past was
I had no idea, I could not remind

A new life started
Days began counting my health
New to every thing around
I tried relishing every hold of my breath

She was my mom and a handsome dad
I was gradually being acquainted to many
Then was equipped with materialistic things
And asked for having aim any

I had a mind blocked and confined
Never was knowing life is one

Still unknown to the world outside
And far from the defeat and won

Ignoring this sphere, I was on routine
That all were tend to make
Parents are support in beginning
And we to soften life for their sake

So life to me seemed like a cycle
Then penetration paved in the books
Turning me practically zero
And at teenage focused on looks

That wasn't all I was motivated and forced
For pursuing a job to earn
Then was married to a girl honestly
Felt myself too prisoned to learn

They, roled as society, we're happy
Though involved complaining a bit
For their definition, now realizing, I have
Brutally spent without revealingly
And with dare enjoying any whit.

The poet loves fire and flame
To show how people treat their shame
Regret & deceived have long queue
Whose justice is forever due

“

There’s a world where mistakes are forgiven

Trust your soul...just

44

Regret Burning Alive

I was a fearsome, a troubling man to be
Cause nothing perfect adorned my life
I had been waiting for some occult such
So I would go without a pensive mind
In fact lifetime is short
Too short for my ambitions
Yet the little could be used as wanted
Cause, fault lies in my body
I was to get all snap clear and wide
And ignored all stupid and waste stuff aside
To be honest, I lost that pleasure
And still was abiding myself
To the busy schedule to console
For all the blames mounting above my head
The sleep of tranquility is never my reach
Cause I am not a happy soul either
I had been complaining all about

And would with an imaginary box of complains indeed
To check out this life, I had paid vast
Yet could not acquire the whole
At the end, I would sit lonely with just the soup bowl
And even if fortunate to get someone with me
I was in draft saving up all my consolations
Because I never befriended death to live life

I'll show how beauty fades too fast
With just a blink of sleeping eyes
That light loses its charm after a spirited dark
Completely turns upside down the night romantic vibes

“

One day, I will be living this day in my memories!

45

Into the Tears

The day brought fate, charming and smooth
And filled my heart and mind with enthusiasm
Adding colors to the surrounding bright
A day ahead I narrated with the same jump of heart
A year hence, with wide grin and lots of excitement
Ten years then, reminisced it like a picture in my album
Later in my life it became a memory of joy
At the end, the first smile of pride and bliss
Turned in tears of the lost memory

“

Now don't blame yourself for anything, my heart...

”

46

Meeting Myself

One day or a night, in an unlisted sight
Standing afore with eyes bright and contacting
And I could position myself to the contact
Linking my mind direction to me, my confidence
Happiness unfolded and eyes recognized
It was me, no the aspiring me
A second later, eyes escaped giving way to red light
Surrounding our extremes
And vibing all set in my heart
Belief flourishing like a red carpet
On which walked my sole satisfaction and sacrifice
Linking myself to what I needed in my heart
What I made grief of was the redness so dull in me
And what it was set to be
Awaiting in the dark my love
Love that I showered
Not that I relished

And I met the core me, my base
Slipping through these, I crashed into my fear
But wasn't hurt, cause the best me had none of it
And this marked my line to be decorated after dizziness.

“

My shadow knew my sins
And the spirit knew all shames
What still provokes this heart
Is someone still making these claims
The fire that thus burst without woods
Seeks to not spread if soil was dry
The shadow hence promised its escape
When I was entering the lights.

“

You need not to wait to heal yourself,
You're healing

47

Deep Breath of Life

Green turns dull and decays being black
Into the soil it needed once to sprout
The death met my happiness and played gamble to deceive
My happiness so blessed raised light of defence
To this bad defeat, death penanced early morning and late night
To revert with the darkest light
To envelope the bliss of my life
And my life so unaware, played in the virtuality of joyous world
And the soul within, heard its feet trembling of my light
Stretched my arms to breathe the deepest and get into the best of me and my life
The deepest breath hugged the darkest light
And the conquest shivered the ground
Suspense washing off excites second by second
Favoring the conquest to the depth of my blessed life

“

Even if the beginning was closed and dull like a bud, don't worry because the result is always a blooming flower...

48

Sharing the Jewel

He sat so down
Turning like the soil on ground
Swinging like dead
On the laughing swing
Depression never laughs
It teases so inhuman
Sets up within the fire to end
And treads the thoughts under its weight
And all the symptoms in my mind
Matched with his position
And I made my mind
Not to help but to hesitate him
Made him feel more down
I stood up a fore
And danced strangely
Teasing the fate and
Enjoying its defamation
I laughed and danced again

Singing broken but melodious song
On spot sung by me
And he still disappointed
But raised his head
Asked me to stop this silly scene
Me, so ignorant resumed my tune
And he kept on stopping me
An hour later he forgot
In stopping me from the silly dance and song
Soon his happy hormone woke up
To meet me, stupid but funny
At the moment
Commanding his body and mind to company me
And he said happily
"I didn't know you came to defy my defeat"
"And deride my death"

The gems and glories
Are to keep framed
To let the outsiders
Know the stories of greatness
The diamond shone from far
Inviting first to itself
The buddies too made a shine
He didn't care for who shone the most,
Took away all not to praise them
To sing another song of greatness

“

And I never wish for the day, lifeless gets life...

49

Soulless

To the lady of this universe
Grandly adorned with vastness of stars
Shinning among the dazzling ways
Slow walk to guard and guide the existence
Meeting the guards of green minds
A humble touch is needed
To green the dried
And she being pensive
Of all excuses and carelessness
Cursed the planet dwellers
Of living a life of dry trees
Innocence sparkled of her raged eyes
Stone on heart and heaviness in voice
She kept on claiming the hurt to soulless
Speechless they, couldn't find guts to guilt
And shattered the pace of merciless cut
Climb and jump to the standing soul

They said lifeless and prioritized their soul
Of greed
The grapes that hugged the tiny twigs
And the nuts spreading on ground
Came to life on hearing the claim
Of the lady
Rose to the fullest voice of pain
Of the trees, flowers and wind
Of what they harmed so cruelly.

“

I did make a call
To the voices unheard
The call was unheard
By those with voice

“

Desiring peace, just get up to work till the last drop of your energy

50

Sweat That Awakes

The noon isn't cool near the pond
Nor the trees have shade to give
Their minds and body,
Weary of loads and hoards,
Of lots of work request to lay
Under the shaded but shadeless tree
Under the cloudy but burning sun
Near the cool but evaporating pond
On the green but pricking grass
Yet they, ignoring all these bad
Rested so peacefully on the aching land
There was no beauty yet seemed a folk
Their sweat of hard work peacefully awoke

“

Who knows if we are already dead,
living now in hell...

51

Meet on Death

Finally I met the river
I had drew water from
While I saw it
I believed that nothing has changed
But the grasses were dull
The trees were thirsty
The animals turned skinny
The people were sick
The sky turned bald
The clouds had ply
The houses were in ruin
Still the river flow so clear and fresh
I could find the river still alive
But the surrounding dead
The blues were yellow
And the dead was me

“

A fantasy beyond...

”

52

From Crown to Ground

Wiping his tears, he, trying to hide his pain
Pain of his dead bride about to leave
Her eye flickering like broken lamp
And tears off her shadow eyes
She knew it was for the last time
A full view of her beloved
Equipped with machines of breath
Life was being injected to lifeless
Body turned pale and skinny
Closing her forever closing eyes
She chose to met death being dead
And holding the hand of his
She persisted on the bed
For the first time, she had hold
Like a princess
Second, when felt the pain
And then scared to gain a feel
His touch could spare this drain

From first he had made feel
She is the crown of his life
And she shinning for loyalty and love
Forever was about to proceed in soil

“

The fall back is pre-written
And the birth is delayed
Death would knock at its time
“Live it to the fullest”, the experiences said

“

I wish the dazzle not to phase off
the world does not need light
The day is enough
The moon shines for its sake and
Not to make us feel its presence...

53

The Stars and Me

The stars and me
Standing aloof and alone
With the time passing and leaves falling
The two separate distanced parallel
Desires still awaits us
For time lent no mercy
The moon guarding those
With vanishing strength and entity
Sometimes letting them face alone
Being hid under clouds
The mountains under the shine
Passing like never existed
But the numbers marked on my skin

“

And if this world ends!
To nature, “end it for peace”

”

54

The Mermaid of Dream

There is always a start
There is always a way
I don't thus mind
I don't thus care
For any such cape
Not a coward
Just blowing a escape
Not a coward
Just meeting a escape
I didn't want to land
The land of hope dwellers
I didn't want to eat
The food of satisfaction
First for all
I wanted grant of my action
And fire up my ambitions
Build up my drives
Suck up my fears

Such types of parallel world
I would rather fold up my arms
And pack up my mind to listen just me
Getting out of ice
Getting rid of fire
Getting off the rain
And breathing in pain
No complains up my shoulders
No dirt up on head
Me heading up to spread the
Drops of myself in rain
Waving my hair and thinking just a dark in shaking
Waiting up for rocks to break my ache
And me swaying like a mermaid in soft water with myself no more fake

“

This glow out of deep happiness
From the small wishes you know
Demanding no light for showing the beauty
The moon has learnt how to glow...

“

I would never believe in being ugly if.........

55

If Mirror Was a Myth

If mirror was a myth
My beauty was blind
And their ugliness was vague
My guilt was false
Surviving without body
And eyes never wet for
Something unthought and untouched
View was their
And though ambiguous but judgments were facts
If mirror was a myth
My confidence was a brave knight massacred in the field of doubt
And my love for myself was peacefully fading
No utterance for such biased motion
And my soul was never to climb a cliff
If mirror was a myth

“

Let the bravest be alive out of consciousness...

”

56

Vague but Value

Shiniest were the pearls
Floating away from the reach
Beyond the setting horizon
And disappearing of their vague impression marked the time run
Which couldn't be captured
In the eyes dazzled by the light of pearls
Around the eyes and eyesight could meet those pearls
But poor were the hands
Tormenting for value
And guilty was the mind overthinking for the value
Unleashed were the abuses for the stupid fate
And brave was the heart to bear the loss

“

This is being crazy, yes, make a judgment...

57

For the Inclined Climb

They are genius indeed
And I can't stop mocking at them
Their positivity is such inclined to well
They feel would bring them water
Dear me, they still incline so much
Craze, greed or need I fail to align
But lastly their hope brings them fall
And hope steps off the embankment
Like me mocking at them

“

Being down is better than feeling down

58

Pleasure Lying Low

I never felt the winds at my feet
never the waves cascading my ankles
It never happened to see
the little ants tickling my toe
neither the grass soothing my sole
For no worry over my head
I never felt the comfort
of loose soil
Yet I feel down
Yet I feel low
Yet I never felt the pleasure
that was always lying low

“

So how would you feel, if one day you see yourself into pieces?

”

59

The Broken Me

I broke a mirror
Thousand pieces apart
And made myself to see the broken me
Weird but my idea was smart
My eye on a piece
And lips on another
My hands were divided brutally
The shiniest me now seemed blur
I bent to uplift
My heart and eyes
The edge touched my tears
Reflecting my dark era of cries
Standing me wasn't suspicious
If the broken parts were broken me
They were laid on ground such
As if my ruins were waiting for sea

“

And the dead dies again!

60

The Dead Head

Even if I walk away forever
My birds won't cry
My dogs won't weep
My flowers would never fade
Off their beauty
My pen would never sink in words
My family won't miss my presence
Adapted to the dead me
That can never force out of the buried soil

For your suggestions and reviews, you can connect to the writer on social media platforms:

1) Facebook
@sunlightraviyadav

2) Instagram
@sunlightraviyadav

3) Mail
sunlightraviyadav@gmail.com

www.ingramcontent.com/pod-product-compliance
Lightning Source LLC
LaVergne TN
LVHW041208150826
845673LV00001B/333

* 9 7 9 8 8 8 8 8 3 2 8 6 8 *